PLATFORM PAPERS

QUARTERLY ESSAYS ON THE PERFORMING ARTS

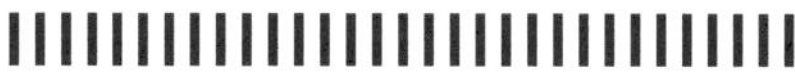

No. 18
October 2008

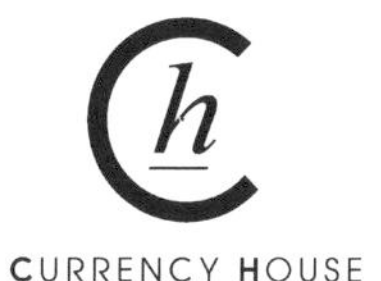

CURRENCY HOUSE

PLATFORM PAPERS
Quarterly essays from Currency House Inc.
Editor: Dr John Golder, j.golder@unsw.edu.au

Currency House Inc. is a non-profit association and resource centre advocating the role of the performing arts in public life by research, debate and publication.

Postal address: PO Box 2270, Strawberry Hills, NSW 2012, Australia
Email: info@currencyhouse.org.au Tel: (02) 9319 4953
Website: www.currencyhouse.org.au Fax: (02) 9319 3649

ISBN 978-0-9802802-8-9
ISSN 1449-583X
Typeset in 10.5 Arrus BT
Printed by Hyde Park Press, Adelaide

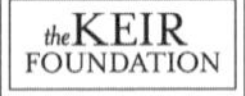

This edition of Platform Papers is supported by the Keir Foundation, the Greatorex Foundation and individual donors. To them and to all our supporters Currency House extends sincere gratitude.

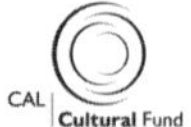

Currency House's touring program is proudly sponsored by the Copyright Agency Limited.

Contents

AVAILABILITY *Platform Papers*, quarterly essays on the performing arts, is published every January, April, July and October and is available through bookshops or by subscription. For order form, see page 78.

LETTERS Currency House invites readers to submit letters of 400–1,000 words in response to the essays. Letters should be emailed to the Editor at info@currencyhouse.org.au or posted to Currency House at PO Box 2270, Strawberry Hills, NSW 2012, Australia. To be considered for the next issue, the letters must be received by 5 November 2008.

CURRENCY HOUSE For membership details, see our website at: www.currencyhouse.org.au

Getting Heard

Achieving an Effective Arts Advocacy

CHRIS PUPLICK

The author

Chris Puplick, AM has a long and passionate involvement with the arts industry, in particular the performing arts and the film industry. He was Liberal Senator for NSW 1979–81, 1984–90, during which time he chaired the Coalition Backbench Committee on Environment and the Arts and was closely associated with such initiatives as the development of the 10BA film tax support scheme. He was Shadow Minister for Environment, Arts, Heritage, Sport, 1987–90.

Post-Parliament he served on the Board of the Griffin Theatre Company for fifteen years including a period as chair, and helped revive the fortunes of that company. He chaired the Freelance Dance Company and was patron and chief financial supporter of the Young at 'Art Theatre Company. He is currently a patron of the Australian Children's Music Foundation. From 1994 he served six years on the Board of NIDA and as a Director of the NIDA Foundation. In 2007 he returned to the Board of NIDA and serves on the Finance Committee.

During his period as Chairman of the Australian National Council on AIDS, Hepatitis C and Related Diseases and as Chair of the AIDS Trust of Australia, Chris took a particular interest in the use of theatre (especially in remote, regional and indigenous communities) as a tool in promoting AIDS education and addressing issues of stigma and discrimination.

In 2007 the Federal Coalition Government appointed

him a member of the Theatre Board of the Australia Council and in 2008 he was appointed by the Labor Government to the inaugural chair of the Board of the newly-independent National Film and Sound Archive,. He also has an extensive interest in museology. He served as a Trustee of the Australian Museum and has published on museums policy.

Chris Puplick has written or co-authored five books, has some ninety publications in Australia and oversea journals and has broadcast extensively as a book reviewer and commentator. He has written and spoken widely on the arts in journals such as the *Canberra Bulletin of Public Administration*, *Overland*, *National Association of the Visual Arts Journal*, *Culture and Policy* and *Southerly*.

Author's acknowledgements

In my research for this essay I discussed their experiences with three former Commonwealth Ministers for the Arts, the Hon. Barry Cohen (1983–87), Senator Hon. Rod Kemp (2001–07) and Senator Hon. George Brandis (2007). I am most grateful for the time they gave me and for their insightful comments. I also benefited from discussions at the Australia Council with Chairman James Strong, AO, Chief Executive Kathy Keele, Executive Director Arts Development Ben Strout and Director of the Theatre Board John Baylis. I acknowledge considerable assistance from the staff at the Library of the Council, particularly Sue Oliver. The Assistant Federal Secretary of the Media Entertainment and Arts Alliance, Simon Whipp, was also generous with his time. Finally, I had the benefit of extensive advice from Justin Macdonnell, author of the standard work on federal arts policy. Naturally, none of the views expressed in this essay should be regarded as other than entirely my own.

Introduction

It does not take much to get the arts onto the front pages of every newspaper and into the public debate across the nation. A prepubescent nipple in a Bill Henson photograph and the subsequent trashing by the Prime Minister of the work of one of Australia's most internationally-respected artists is all it takes. So is a photograph of the same prime minister, armed with flowers, at the maternal bedside of one of our most luminescent stars—while his Labor Party colleagues are paying their respects at the funeral of one of their most beloved stalwarts. Court proceedings are always good for a headline: disputes over the awarding of an Archibald Prize or attempts by Church groups to revive laws about blasphemy so as to ban a play or a film.

For the more economically-minded, perhaps it is the news that yet another record price has been paid for a painting bought or sold in Australia.[1] It's hard to forget the public outcry when the Whitlam Government paid over $1 million for *Blue Poles*—in light of the painting's current value, perhaps the most fiscally responsible decision that government ever made.

Then, of course, there are the human stories: how the Poms gave Ross Stretton such a horrible time at the Royal Ballet, not, heaven forbid, because he was finding it too hard to manage, but because he was only a 'colonial'.[2] And, at the end of the day, there will always be headlines about another star/potential star found dead of an overdose of legal/illicit drugs, or some other moron's boorish behaviour on yet another mindless reality TV show, followed by a prime ministerial denunciation and threats to change broadcasting standards.

Despite the fine body of arts writers, critics, analysts and commentators which Australia can boast, despite the high level of academic and intellectual study in both our universities and ever-declining ranks of serious journals; despite the unbounded talents of our arts practitioners themselves, the engendering of serious public debate about the arts and about arts funding is an almost impossible task in our contemporary community.

This essay will concentrate on a single aspect of this public debate: the public funding of the performing arts and, in particular, the provision of public funds through one-off political or parliamentary initiatives, or else the funding of the Australia Council. *It asks both how and why these funding decisions were made and, above all, who has influenced their making.*

My thesis will be that the levels of support for the arts and the development of initiatives and new directions are a function not of public demand for the arts or the products of the arts industry (loosely defined), and that they are certainly not a function of the advocacy role or skills of Australian arts professionals or practitioners. Rather, it will be argued, the critical factors have been the *personal* support lent by senior political leaders, prominent and well-connected business leaders, or senior bureaucrats with a interest in particular art forms.

It may well be said that in this context the survival and growth of the arts sector in Australia is essentially dependent upon the kindness of strangers.

Consequently, what I want to explore in these pages is the question of how to find the right strangers. Where are they lurking and how do we entice them out of their lairs? What can they do when they do emerge and what is the cost of such an exercise?

1

Making policy

Arts policy in Australia, or rather policy about selective issues in the arts, has always been made in the absence of a national arts strategy or policy. Whether or not this is a good thing is open to debate.

In an earlier Platform Paper David Throsby asked whether Australia needs a cultural policy. His conclusion was to reject the idea of a 'magisterial cultural statement' imposed from above by a prime minister, cabinet or parliament, and to support 'the opening up of a broad-ranging discussion about the role of the arts and culture in our society, and the forging of a new cultural accord between government and people'.[3]

To a certain extent it could be argued that this was the approach taken in October 1994 by *Creative Nation*, which purported to be a statement of 'Commonwealth Cultural Policy' and was the result of deliberations by a panel of eminent Australians drawn widely from within the arts and creative industries who had been appointed by the Government in July 1992. The whole *Creative Nation* initiative was the brain-child of Prime Minister Paul Keating, who had positioned himself as a champion of the higher arts through a number of personal initiatives, including the creation of the Australian Artists Creative Fellowships.[4] Neither *Creative Nation* nor the Fellowship scheme survived the change of government in 1996, and so the impact of the former, with its bold assertions and commitments to improving the cultural life of the nation, came to nothing.

Indeed, *Creative Nation* prompted much critical analysis within the arts community[5] and was roundly derided in some quarters for its assertions such as the following: 'The ultimate aim of this cultural policy is to increase the comfort and enjoyment of Australian life',[6] which Barrie Kosky scorned as 'the role of furniture and restaurants',[7] and appeared to be little different from the subsequent Prime Minister John Howard's vision of Australia as a nation which was 'relaxed and comfortable'.

Given that governments have effectively eschewed further attempts to create comprehensive national arts or cultural policies, and that, as a result, decisions about the arts tend to be made in isolation and without regard for any master-plan, I would like to explore what

I believe have been the three fundamental sources of arts policies or initiatives.

As a preliminary, I should state my own interests and credentials in this matter. I have had the unique advantage of operating on all three sides of the funding/policy triangle: as a policy maker, as a mendicant and as a funder. From 1978 to 1981 and from 1984 to 1990 I was a Senator in the Federal Parliament. In the earlier period I chaired the (Fraser) Government's backbench committee responsible for environment and arts matters, working with several ministers. It was this backbench committee which was responsible for the approval of the 10BA film funding arrangements and which oversaw a number of arts initiatives undertaken by Minister Bob Ellicott. From 1987 to 1990 I was in the Shadow Cabinet with portfolios for the Environment, Arts, Heritage, Sport and the Bicentennial. Since then I have served on, and chaired, the Board of the Griffin Theatre Company, the Freeland Dance Company, and currently I serve on the Board of the National Institute of Dramatic Art (NIDA) and as the inaugural chair of the Board of the National Film and Sound Archive. I am also a member of the Theatre Board of the Australia Council and was chair of a private philanthropic trust which provided financial grants to individual artists. Having been involved in 'arts policy' both at a policy-maker level and at the level of both seeking and allocating funds, I have had the opportunity to observe the interplay of these competing roles at first hand.

2

Policy by (passing) interest

I have already mentioned the establishment of the Australian Artists Creative Fellowships, which were the personal initiative of Paul Keating. Two points are worth noting here. In the first instance, it was widely reported that the impetus for the creation of this support scheme came from Keating's 'shocked' discovery that Geoffrey Tozer, an internationally reputed Liszt pianist, 'earned $9,000 a year as his son's music teacher and rode a bike to work, while his [Keating's] 18-year-old secretary earned $32,000'.[8] One cannot but note that the well-known low level of income for professional artists and the advantages of riding a bike to work appear to have come as a surprise to the then Treasurer, but not to most people knowledgeable about arts matters.

The second point about the Fellowship scheme was that in its original iteration, writers were excluded from consideration on the basis of Keating's belief that literature was not 'art' in the same way that music, theatre, dance or painting were. This exclusion was reversed once a telephone call to the Treasurer had been made by the then Chair of the Australia Council, Professor Donald Horne.[9]

In this respect, the Keating Fellowships scheme harks back directly to May 1908 and the first Commonwealth Government initiative in support of the arts, the Commonwealth Literary Fund, established in May 1908.[10] The genesis of this fund, which provided grants of up to £500 'for the relief of indigent authors', arose when poet and satirist Victor Daly died in December 1905 leaving his widow and family in dire straits. In June 1906 H.B. Higgins—who was later to deliver the celebrated Harvester Judgement—raised this individual case in the Federal Parliament where a sympathetic Prime Minister Alfred Deakin promised to investigate the matter. Once a committee of distinguished citizens had considered the broad policy question involved and reported favourably in support of an 'Australian Men of Letters Fund', the Commonwealth Literary Fund came into existence.[11]

This is the recurring pattern of Australian arts policy. An individual case sparks interest in a sympathetic political leader (at the highest level), perhaps with some prodding from senior arts administrators, and action is forthcoming. It was replicated in 1938, when the Commonwealth Literary Fund was extended to assist in the publication of outstanding manuscripts in creative writing and the subsidy of university lectures in Australian literature;[12] and again in 1912, with the creation of the Commonwealth Art Advisory Board to make recommendations on the commissioning of portraits and the purchase of paintings for the national collection.[13]

The same pattern of policy development continued with Prime Minister Menzies' enthusiastic embrace of an Australian Elizabethan Theatre Trust to mark the Queen's first Royal Visit in 1954;[14] and Prime Minister Holt's sponsorship of the Commonwealth Assistance to Australian Composers scheme in 1967. Again, it was Menzies' personal interest which led to the passing of the *National Library Act* in 1960, separating that body from the Parliamentary Library.

Enter Dr H.C. ('Nugget') Coombs. Coombs had been chair of the Trust from 1954 and was already known as Australia's most distinguished public servant, indeed, perhaps Australia's first public intellectual. With the retirement of Menzies and the accession of Harold Holt as Prime Minister a new era in arts policy opened. It was Coombs who persuaded a sympathetic Prime Minister to replace the Australian Elizabethan Theatre Trust as the Government's principal arts funding authority with an Australian Council for the Arts—later to become today's Australia Council. It was left to Holt's successor, John Gorton, to complete this arrangement. Coombs was the chair of the Council 1968–74. He was succeeded by Professor Peter Karmel who oversaw the conversion to the Australia Council in 1975, the model having been designed by Coombs himself.

Interested parties and sympathetic politicians combined again in 1968/9 when Barry Jones, Phillip Adams and Peter Coleman were instrumental in persuading Prime Minister Gorton to lend financial support to the Australian film industry and set in train plans for the establishment of the National Film and Television School. What attracted Gorton to this policy was less an interest in the arts for their own sake than an understanding of the role of the arts in fostering Australian nationalism, a subject which was the hallmark of Gorton's philosophy and style of political leadership.[15]

This need to protect a unique version of what it means to be Australian and to export that to the rest of the world was equally evident in the personal support given by Arts Minister Bob Ellicott in the Fraser Government to a plan to encourage the growth of the Australian film industry by the introduction of significant taxation incentives. Ellicott's support came in two tranches. The first, introduced in 1978, was section 10B of the Income Tax Act which allowed money invested in film production to be claimed as a tax deduction over the two years following the release of the film. After some concerns had been expressed by Treasurer John Howard, and threats made to act retrospectively against what was claimed to be a series of film industry 'bottom of the harbour' tax avoidance schemes, Ellicott moved to clarify his policies. Just prior to the 1980 election he announced a new film investment scheme of even greater generosity but with some more coherent rules attached. This was referred to as section 10BA.[16] In this he 'not only outmanoeuvred the emergent dries in Cabinet, and in the Treasury'[17] but established himself as a leading force in Australia's cultural environment.

Although there was some lobbying from film producers to achieve a yet-more-favourable tax regime for film investment, there was little contact between individual artists and the Government[18] and the successful introduction of the scheme was a personal triumph for Ellicott in the face of strong opposition from the Treasury. Sadly, as Justin Macdonnell observes of the 10BA scheme:

> Thought up in the white heat of the campaign trail, it became one of the most generous allowances to any industry anywhere in the Western world. As such it carried within it the seeds of its own destruction.[19]

Ellicott's other major achievement as Minister for Home Affairs was to carry the Coalition Party Room to support the building of the New Parliament House—again in the face of trenchant opposition from both the Treasury and Prime Minister Fraser himself. In all the time I served in that Party Room the decision to build the New Parliament House was the only one put to an actual vote and carried against the Prime Minister's wishes. As part of his argument in favour of the new building Ellicott stressed the extent to which the building itself would be a major impetus for the development of the arts in Australia, ranging from the furniture and craft industries, through tapestry-making and the development of new art works; the capacity to display parts of the national collections throughout the building and the employment of skilled craftspeople in every stage of the building's construction. The impact of this investment in a new public building is often overlooked in discussions about how the arts and craft industries are supported.

Successive governments have continued to give generous financial support packages for the arts, most recently in the form of the producers' offset scheme, introduced by Liberal Arts Minister Rod Kemp in the

2007 federal budget.[20] Kemp was fascinated by the fact that when he was engaged in discussions about the film industry with their representatives, there were only two issues which seemed to be of the slightest concern to them, 'tax and quotas'. Given the extent to which these, rather than artistic issues, tend to shape that industry, such a situation is hardly surprising.

Rod Kemp recently remarked to me that his success as 'the burglar of the budget'—a reference by his Departmental Secretary to his having extracted over $1 billion for the arts during his five years as Minister for the Arts—was predicated on his being a close friend of the then Treasurer, Peter Costello. As Kemp tells it, the general process of arts policy-making was for the Minister to work up a proposal, and to 'run it past' Prime Minister Howard. Given that the Prime Minister was not particularly exercised about arts matters and that the sums of money being requested were miniscule within the overall context of the Budget, Howard's attitude was inclined to be, 'If you can sort it out with the Treasurer, then you can have it.' The Minister then approached his friend and generally got away with it.

Occasionally, politicians do have 'vision'. A recent report on the efforts of architect Jan Utzon to further the original vision of his father Joern in the refurbishment of the Sydney Opera House contained this statement:

> Joe Cahill (the NSW Premier who approved the Opera House project) said to my father, 'I'm not a particular opera or theatre goer but I'm in charge of the city, and a city like Sydney should have the

> facilities of a capital city in Europe. There are people who like swimming and football; these things all have facilities in Sydney. But there are none for music other than the Town Hall. We must have these facilities to make the city liveable in the full sense.[21]

The impetus given to the developments of the arts in South Australia during the Premiership of Don Dunstan (1967–78 and 1970–79) is well known and widely recognised. The extent to which this proceeded from Dunstan's own personal interest and commitments is equally appreciated. So much so, that when current Western Australian Premier Alan Carpenter made a major announcement about enhanced arts funding in his State, he proclaimed, 'I sort of see myself as Don Dunstan minus the shorts. You only have this chance once as a Premier.' The chance to which he was referring was a massive injection of $73 million into the arts sector late in 2007. At the time Carpenter stated, 'There are no votes in the arts, but you have to do it anyway.' Citing the names of numerous leading Western Australian arts practitioners, the Premier went on, in terms reminiscent of the underlying mantras of *Creative Nation*:

> There are these great talented people we can hold up, shine up and help develop their talents and present to the world and make life more interesting.[22]

So, the personal sense of the centrality of the arts to civic life and the commitment of serious financial support by Premiers Cahill, Dunstan and Carpenter have all left their mark on their respective States and beyond. Without them, we must ask, would the outcomes have been the same?

3

Policy by (public) inquiry

Almost no area of public policy seems as replete with Inquiries as arts policy in Australia, and no area of policy seems to have been more shaped by the outcomes of inquiries.[23] Although not part of this paper's consideration, the area of arts/cultural policy which best exemplifies this is that of broadcasting.[24] Starting with the 1928 Royal Commission on Wireless (the Hammond Inquiry) there followed a further nine public inquiries which helped shape the broadcasting structures and environment of today. (A list of these inquiries is given in the Appendix.)

Elsewhere in the arts sector there have been at least 18 major public inquiries encompassing everything from Indigenous arts and crafts, to Folklife, to orchestras, to arts training, to museums and of course to arts funding arrangements. In addition to these reports, the Australia Council has produced a huge corpus of work dealing with aspects of the arts sector encompassing issues such as the marketing of Aboriginal artefacts, public support for and attitudes towards the arts, the development of music theatre, studies of the earnings of professional artists and the development of theatre for young people. Equally, it should be noted that the Australia Council itself, like the Australian Broadcasting Corporation, has been the subject of numerous inquiries and reviews, both by parliamentary committees and by external reviewers such as McKinsey and Co.

Finally, I would draw attention to the vast number of inquiries that have been held into aspects of intellectual property and copyright law, including significant issues for artists such as those touching on moral rights and resale royalties.

The scope and impact of these inquiries has varied enormously. A report such as that by the Vincent Committee (1964), although its recommendations were unwelcome and ignored by the government at the time, effectively established the basis upon which the Australian television production industry was eventually encouraged and supported; the Piggott Inquiry (1974) set the broad direction for the development of museums in Australia and the Nugent Inquiry (1999) fundamentally reshaped the way in which performing arts organisations are funded, although it did not question the organisational structures themselves.

On the other hand, the Fraser Government rejected out of hand the recommendations of the Industries Assistance Commission report of 1976. This was an ill-conceived inquiry in the wake of perceived Whitlam largesse, to which witnesses attempted to make a special pleading for the arts, but failed to persuade the commissioners of the benefits. The interesting National Inquiry into Folklife was simply ignored, its 51 recommendations disappearing into the black hole of departmental apathy.[25] Some of the inquiries were responses to highly-charged political debates, such as the Carroll Inquiry (2003) into alleged bias in the (mainly Aboriginal) content of the National Museum of Australia, and others were attempts to solve pressing financial and funding problems, such as the Tribe (1985) and Strong (2005) reports into orchestras. However, what is of most significant note is that none of the inquiries arose from anything which could be described as concerted pressure from practitioners or industry/sector representatives—although the Eggleston Inquiry did take place against a background of media stories about the exploitation of Indigenous artists and their work.

These inquiries almost always occur when governments discern that a problem is arising and that advice from external experts is more likely to yield practical and politicly-acceptable outcomes than internal deliberations. The reports from the Australia Council, on the other hand, have largely focused on the immediate concerns of the Council or its Boards and the need to address problems of immediate relevance. In recent years the Council's reports have begun to address more long-term and strategic issues.

On balance, we must conclude that major developments in national arts policy (especially in the funding area) have been shaped primarily by these series of inquiries, and, although almost all of them have been the result of extensive public input (by way of submissions and hearings), the driving force in each has been the chairperson and the political sponsor of the initial reference.

4

Policy by (political) influence

It is clear from even a cursory examination of the arts policy developments outlined above that the role of individuals of particular, especially political, influence has been critical in the way in which policy development has been shaped. Higgins' intervention with Deakin prompted the Commonwealth Literary Fund; Coombs intervention with Holt and Gorton precipitated the forerunner of the Australia Council; Adams, Jones and Coleman persuaded Gorton to start the Commonwealth's significant involvement with the film industry; Horne's intervention with Keating shaped the Australian Artists Creative Fellowships and David Barnett's criticisms of the Australian Museum foreshadowed the Carroll Inquiry.

Special pleading, of course, is in direct contravention of the central philosophy of government arts funding, namely the 'arm's-length' principle. (This principle was once described to me by a highly-experienced observer of the arts scene as the principle of 'keeping artists as far away from Ministers as possible—for the sake of both their healths'.)

The classic example of the success of special pleading was the decision of the Fraser Government in 1977 to reserve to itself the right to determine the level of funding for the Australian Ballet, Australian Opera and the Australian Elizabethan Theatre Trust by way of what is known as 'one-line' direct funding in the annual Budget. This decision (strongly opposed by the Australia Council itself [26]) came about as a result of dissatisfaction by the 'big three' companies with the level of funding being allocated by the Australia Council and a view which their leadership put to the Fraser Ministry that the Commonwealth had a special responsibility to support 'excellence' and 'flagship companies'—by implication at least, against the assaults of the somehow less worthy or lower quality competitors.[27]

The removal of funding responsibility for these major organisations from the Council to the Cabinet was a lobbying coup by the Chairs of both the Opera and the Ballet. Historically, these two major companies had been led by some of the most prominent Sydney and Melbourne business identities, men of impeccable financial and political connections (such as Sir Robert Southey at the Australian Ballet, who was a long-time Federal President of the Liberal Party, and Donald McDonald, general manager first of the Sydney Theatre Company, then of the Australian Opera, who was at one time chairman of John Howard's campaign committee in his Federal seat of Bennelong and subsequently Howard's appointment as Chairman of the Australian Broadcasting Corporation).

Special pleading decisions continued until the Australia Council resolved a more effective structure to deal with the tensions arising from the funding competition between the major companies and the small-to-medium organisations. This became a more urgent issue to address with the decision of the Hawke Labor Government in 1983–84 to abandon one-line funding and return responsibility for the big three organisations' funding to the Australia Council.

Disputes over funding allocations led to the suggestion by the Theatre Board (but not the Music Board) to consider a system of 'ceiling funding' on the major companies in order to allow growth money to be directed to the rest of the performing arts sector.[28] This debate led, at the same time, to a major split, and the effective demise of the national Confederation of Australian Professional Performing Arts (CAPPA) which was unable to resolve the tensions between its competing constituents. In the event, after the prompting of the McLeay Report (1987), and the formal recommendation in *Creative Nation*, for the establishment of a Major Organisations Board, such a body (wonderfully known as 'the MOB') was established by the Australia Council in April 1995. The MOB morphed into the Major Performing Arts Board as a result of a further refinement of its operations by the Nugent Inquiry.

Former Arts Minister Barry Cohen has commented on this whole special pleading phenomenon. When you first inherit the arts portfolio, he says, various arts companies and heavyweights descend, demanding a commitment to the principle of arms-length funding. No sooner is this given, than the same entities round on you with reasons why their own company/art form is worthy of special treatment and specific assistance.

The same thing, I can report from personal experience, happens even with Shadow Ministers.

Cohen himself was by no means averse to stacking his boards or instructing the funding authorities (in particular the Australia Council) in government policy preferences and commitments, and making it clear that he would have no hesitation in intervening in funding allocations,[29] as indeed he had the legal right to do as Minister.

Cohen's letter to the Australia Council accompanying details of the 1985 Budget allocation drew attention to the Council's 'special responsibility' to fund the Australian Ballet, the Australian Opera and the Australian Elizabethan Theatre Trust orchestras. (This approach was endorsed by the recommendation of the McLeay Report, when it recommended that 'the three largest clients' of the Council (AB/AO/AETT) should be funded separately on a triennial basis, a recommendation endorsed by both the Council itself and the Government.[30])

A more recent example was the Howard Government's provision of an exceptional amount of additional funding ($19.4 million) to the small and medium theatre sector. Although need for such funding had clearly been identified by the March 2002 report to Cultural Ministers,[31] little action had resulted. It was James Strong, Chair of the Australia Council, who obtained a private meeting with Prime Minister Howard and persuaded him of the need for this significant additional funding. This additional funding allowed the Council's Theatre Board to develop its radical plans for reshaping of funding allocations within this sector through the *Make It New* initiative of April 2006. Without Strong's personal intervention these extra funds are unlikely to have been forthcoming.

Yet again, one can cite the decision during the dying days of the Howard Government to provide an additional sum of $1.5 million to bail out the financially-troubled Sydney Dance Company. This was not the first occasion on which this company had found itself in financial strife and had its special pleading rewarded by the Federal Government. While the special status of the SDC,[32] and the national 'need' to keep it afloat, is something one can argue, the truth of the matter is that, in the heat of the 2007 Federal Election campaign, Arts Minister George Brandis had put to the Prime Minister the case for two one-off grants: to the SDC and the National Institute of Dramatic Art (NIDA). The Prime Minister, using delegated authority that did not require him to bring the matter to Cabinet, agreed to the payment of one but not the other.

Although all governments assert their support of the arms-length funding principle,[33] this was always a compromised policy. In the first instance, Government controls the purse-strings. There is no guaranteed independent source of arts funding (such as the British Broadcasting Corporation has with the revenue from television licence fees) and governments can use global budget allocations to influence funding outcomes.

Secondly, Government always has the power of patronage in terms of who it appoints to the Australia Council (and indeed to other funding organisations such as the Australian Research Council, which funds many of the academic research initiatives in the arts) and any other governing Board or funding authority. Cabinet has to approve the appointment of members of the Council itself and the Minister has the power to appoint the members of the individual art-form Boards which allocate funds directly.

Thirdly, there are always election campaign promises about new arts investment or initiatives. The promise of a regional art gallery, one-off payments for individual projects or companies, new support schemes, taxation incentives or support for changes in local content rule, resale royalty or copyright legislation often pop out during the course of these regularly-occurring national events. For example, at the 2007 election, ALP policy pledged that the National Film and Sound Archive would be established as an independent statutory authority. This followed its separation from the Australian Film Commission, an initiative which had been trenchantly resisted by the previous Coalition Government. The ALP also promised to implement a resale royalty scheme for visual artists—again a matter not encouraged by the Coalition.[34]

Fourthly, the government of the day may choose to create new and special ways of injecting additional funding into the arts. To celebrate the centenary of Australia's federation, the Howard Government established the Centenary of Federation Fund. A total of $1 billion was appropriated for this initiative. The arts sector was a beneficiary of some of this largesse, for example the Stage Two development of NIDA, the country's leading theatre training institution, was funded to the tune of $25 million, and $7 million was committed to commence construction of the National Museum of Australia. In 2002/03 more than $280 million was spent from the Fund on a series of regional arts initiatives such as support for the Gunnedah Performing Arts Centre, the Australian Museum of Flight at Nowra, and the Australian Prospectors and Miners Hall of Fame in Kalgoorlie. Decisions about allocation from the Fund were made at ministerial level with no pretence that the arms-length principle should apply without qualification.

Interestingly, the resulting confrontation between Minister Cohen and the Australia Council over his 1985 letter—which was resolved, inevitably, by the Council climbing down from its high ground of objecting to any form of ministerial 'guidance'—led to a concerted effort by arts practitioners to organise themselves into some sort of effective lobby group.[35]

This was the creation of the Arts Alliance. It had as its members the National Association of Visual Arts (NAVA), the Art Workers Union, the Crafts Council of Australia, Actors Equity, the Musicians Union,[36] CAPPA,[37] the Association of Community Theatres, the Australian Theatrical and Amusement Employees Association, the Australian Writers Guild and the Producers and Directors Guild of Australia. Although claiming membership of some 65,000,[38] and even on one occasion organising a day of protest by artists across the nation, the Arts Alliance had little practical effect on the development or outcomes of arts policy and soon faded.

Broadcasting policy, fortunately beyond the scope of this paper, is another area replete with evidence of how national policy is made through personal influence. Questions of licence issue and renewal, in the days before this was done by an independent statutory authority, reveal a system of personal favouritism. As applications came before Cabinet for approval, the questions of cross-media ownership, restrictions on licence-reach and the introduction or deferral of new technologies are very much the interplay of a small number of key Ministers and an equally small number of media moguls (plus their vast array of highly-paid lobbyists). Whether it is policy by interest, policy by inquiry or policy by influence, it is clearly not policy by constituents, consumers or practitioners.

Jennifer Radbourne's summary of policy development over the period from 1945 to 1990 remains true to this day. 'Individuals of influence', she wrote of 1945, 'continued to shape the Commonwealth arts funding mechanism, possibly strengthened by the constant criticism, investigation and inquiry.'[39]

5

Outcomes

Radbourne defines this very Australian approach to policy development in the following way:

> Documentation of the historical evidence demonstrates that the catalyst for development, change, growth, challenge and innovation in performing arts

> practice in Australia has been a dual consequence of individual vision and considerable sustenance by the Commonwealth Government. In every phase of growth a particular individual (Coombs, Hunt, Battersby, Pascoe, Whitlam, Staley, Horne, Yerbury) has stimulated thought and action in government decision-makers and gathered momentum in finding support to encourage the Australian arts community to act and grow in performance and management function.

She goes on:

> The 'arts community' comprises three groups of people: those who are practitioners, performers, participants in the arts experience: those who form the arts 'élite', that is the establishment, the decision makers, with power over the practitioners: and finally the individuals who have a sympathy and vision for the arts, together with significant skill as persuaders of governments, exemplified particularly by H.C. Coombs and Donald Horne.[40]

This judgement is supported by Jennifer Craik's comment on arts policy under the Howard Government:

> Overall, there was no vision for the arts and culture [...] Instead, the Government placed its bets on the 'Big End' of town—national cultural organisations that were visible, élite-oriented and represented by effective lobbyists.[41]

While I would take issue with some part of Craik's assessment, since the latter part of the Howard Government saw significant investment in the small-to-medium sector of the arts community, I do agree that there was a preference for dealing only with the major players and with accommodating the demands of effective lobbyists as a way of determining what might pass for 'arts policy'. Indeed, a more accurate assessment of the outcomes of these policy approaches asserts that

> [t]hrough its review-driven cultural agenda the Howard Government has given the arts greater funding than most governments. Its record for injecting extra funds into the arts is impressive, up there with the Whitlam, Keating, Kennett (Victoria) and Dunstan (South Australia) administrations.[42]

6

Finding the right strangers

If my analysis of the origins of arts policy and funding decisions is correct, then clearly arts advocates need to identify and develop their 'friends at court'—they need to find those strangers upon whose kindness they can depend. I would distinguish two classes of strangers here: the first being the members of Parliament and the Ministry who can be of assistance, and the second being those individuals outside the parliamentary realm who have influence upon policy makers.

Within the Parliament, allies are needed both at the Ministerial and the backbench levels. Obviously, Arts Ministers themselves (and increasingly their key staff advisors) are a prime target. Arts Ministers vary in both their enthusiasm for the portfolio—some, after all, did not seek the job, but rather had it thrust upon them—and their ranking in the political pecking-order. Sometimes Arts Ministers are in Cabinet, usually they are not. However, Arts Ministers are often the least powerful players in this game. Prime Ministers get interested in the arts from time to time. Some of them are real enthusiasts; some get occasional bursts of interest in particular art forms or events; others prefer a day at the races. The Treasurer and the Minister for Finance play vital roles: usually the sums of money involved in arts expenditure are so insignificant that a nod from the Treasurer may be all that is required. Occasionally, a Foreign Affairs Minister may have a role in arts policy matters when this is seen as enhancing Australia's diplomacy in a particular direction or in with a particular nation. Education Ministers may turn out to be a major source of financing for the arts through a variety of programs; and increasingly the holder of the Communications portfolio—especially if the ABC and SBS are funded in this area, or if production and broadcast quotas are at issue—are players in this game. Ministers with responsibility for rural or regional development and ministers for Indigenous affairs all have a variety of interests in the arts and a varying capacity to provide both political support and funding.

Beyond the front benches lie the vast reaches of the backbench, usually crowded with ministerial hopefuls all seeking some way to make their mark. Key positions are occupied by the chairs of the relevant portfolio committees. Arts advocates need to know who these individuals are, to have some sense of whether they have political clout, and what their personal pressure points might be.

Personal knowledge, gained by proper due diligence, is vital. By way of example, when I was Shadow Minister for the Environment, Parliament debated measures to ban chlorofluorocarbons (CFCs) from the atmosphere. Both sides wanted to be as tough as possible—to out-macho each other. A proposal was advanced to allow a major exemption from the CFC ban for certain chemical and pharmaceutical companies. The Opposition was not impressed with this exemption until the industry lobbyist involved reminded me that my asthma puffer was powered by CFCs and asked me how comfortable I personally would be (not to mention my constituents) with those devices being withdrawn from the market. Point made and taken!

So, it's important to know what interest each key parliamentarian (and, indeed, their family members) has in the arts. Are they regular attendees? Do they take their kids to ballet? Do they represent electorates where rural arts activities are strong (local museums, musical societies, art galleries etc)? Knowledge about their families may be important. It was well known that Malcolm Fraser's daughter Phoebe was an activist in support of whale protection, and that this had a significant impact on his thinking during the debate in 1980 which led to Australia switching from being a whale-hunting nation to a leader of the whale-conservation movement. Jeanette Howard took a particular interest in some of the costume design and making work at NIDA while Thérèse Rein has recently evidenced great interest in the work of the National Film and Sound Archive.

Influence must extend across the political divide. When arts funding or policy becomes a matter of controversy the outcome is inevitable. No government will expend its political capital in support of something controversial where it is perceived that there are 'no votes'. It will not risk alienating the general public over what can be portrayed as special favours for élites—or, worse, for the politically/socially outrageous. *Thus arts advocates have to have the Opposition on side with their cause.* I have been most critical of those arts advocates and unions who make ideological assumptions that only one side of politics cares about the arts. *Political power is always shared in Australia and this fact needs to be recognised.*

Outside the realm of Parliament itself there are always people in business and public life who make effective arts advocates. Many do this by being major donors, but most are chosen because they have gained political access through credentials other than the arts. Once persuaded to become advocates for a particular art form or company, they may, in turn, chair a major inquiry (Myer, Nugent), be appointed chair of a major national institution (Stokes, McDonald), be a major force in the economic debates about arts funding (Eslake) or even chair a major funding organisation (Strong).

Again, getting to these major players is in itself an art, and the contact point is often through a member of their family (think Murdoch, Pratt, Packer). It's a matter of knowing what they are interested in and what they are prepared to do. Knowing the right buttons to push is critical. There can be any number of these: promoting Australian nationalism or identity; contributing to regional development or employment; enhancing multiculturalism or reconciliation; supporting international initiatives; enhancing health or educational outcomes; promoting social or physical rehabilitation; adding to economic growth or revenue; raising/creating a positive personal or corporate profile or even, if all else fails—*ars gratia artis*. What these friends at court can do is not so much to deliver money (other than their own) or outcomes, but rather to help open doors and create environments in which arts advocacy with the real decision-makers in government is facilitated.

All this begs the question: what's in it for them? In his *An Economic Theory of Democracy*, Anthony Downs makes the point that putting in great effort for minimal return is an irrational activity, and so the rational thing to do is to leave it to others. Leave aside the question of genuine interest or altruism—which, contrary to many claims, exists in large measure—and just focus on the question uppermost in the mind of any politician: *How do I get re-elected?* When arts advocates ask for something, they need to offer more in return than simply to say that they will always be grateful. Public recognition of a job well done is a start.

Public recognition does not have to be much. Circulars, letters, newsletters to supporters or members acknowledging the role of the individual concerned; letters to the editors of local papers; the conferring of honorary membership or patronage; regular invitations to functions; recognition in programs and annual reports—all these gestures are potentially meaningful. They should also be long-term, and extend beyond the supporter's retirement from formal positions. (I still remember being unceremoniously dropped from the Australian Opera's invitation list the moment I ceased to be Shadow Minister.) All this requires thought, planning, research, due diligence, on the part of the arts advocate, an understanding of how the political system works and an appreciation of the constraints under which it and the people within it operate. It requires the expenditure of time and an approach of sensitivity.

I had the unique experience of being both Chairman of the key backbench committee in Government and Shadow Minister for the Environment and the Arts when in Opposition, so was responsible for policy in both areas at the same time. Needless to say, I was lobbied by both interests. In relation to the environment I was rarely approached by individuals. On almost every occasion it was a peak body: the Australian Conservation Foundation, Project Jonah, the International Fund for Animal Welfare, Friends of the Earth. With the arts, on the other hand, the approaches were personal and individual (or individual arts companies or institutions). The delegates were never from peak groups. Further, the environment advocates always began by painting the big picture: they saw beyond their own immediate needs (which of course they pushed strongly) and recognised that other environmental issues were equally vital and funding needed to be increased for everybody. Arts advocates, on the other hand, rarely looked beyond their own interests, were even happy to recommend where other bodies' funding might be cut. They almost never went into bat for a larger arts allocation for all.

In my experience, genuine respect and dialogue between parliamentarians and arts lobbyists was often in short supply. Politicians too often regard arts advocates as cultural élitists who despise the process of politics and think their arguments should be accepted for their self-evident validity. They wonder why arts advocates can't see that the magic pudding simply doesn't exist. Meanwhile their constituents want to know why money that is being spent on opera, lesbian drum festivals, or acquiring another Jackson Pollock, is not being spent on their children's school or their neighbourhood hospital. In a democracy our elected representatives want to hear from arts advocates who understand a few of these basic principles.

On the other hand the arts advocate wants to be able to talk to a politician who is concerned with more than immediately measurable things, or issues popular with the tabloids or in the toxic swamp of talk-back radio. They want to engage with people who are, after all, in significant national leadership positions and who have some sense of the wider social values of art and culture. They want to engage with a politician who would be as hesitant to cut funding to the National Gallery as s/he would to the War Graves Commission, recognising the deeper value which both of those institutions have beyond the immediate and the tangible.

More often than not what separates these parties is not any really meaningful disagreement about values but rather an inability to use mutually comprehensible and understandable language. A prime example in this regard is the extent to which politicians talk about 'outcomes' whereas artists and institutions are absorbed with the process of art. They simply do not see themselves as being in the business of producing outcomes. In this, I am afraid to say, it is the arts advocates who must yield. It is they who need to talk the language of politics and to frame their cases in the currency of political debate.

7

Where have the artists been?

If artists themselves or their representative organisations have not been to the forefront in the determination of national arts policy, where have they been? The answer is, of course, that they have been hard pressed supporting their arts practice. Studies by David Throsby and others have made it clear that the earnings of most professional artists are small; that most in the performing arts spend a significant portion of the time out of work and that both time and opportunity for participation in activities such as political organisation and lobbying are at a premium.[43] The record of Australian artists, particularly in the performing arts sector, in organising and sustaining peak national lobby groups or associations has not been impressive.

Nevertheless, Australia is not without a variety of major arts lobby groups.

The film industry has been particularly successful in developing and sustaining a number of such groups. These include the three major government-supported organisations, the Film Finance Corporation, the Australian Film Commission and Film Australia—all now being brought together under the aegis of Screen Australia. In addition the Screen Producers Association of Australia, Ausfilm and the smaller bodies associated with the National Film, and Sound Archive (the Archive Forum and the Friends of the Archive) all exist to promote various aspects of film industry policy to government.

In print, the Australian Writers' Guild, the Australian Society of Authors and the Australian Publishers' Association cover a variety of interests. Museums and collecting institutions sustain the Collections Council of Australia and Museums Australia. The music industry has the Australian Performing Right Association (APRA), the Australian Record Industry Association (ARIA), the Australian Children's Music Foundation, the Australian Music Centre, and the Music Council of Australia.

The visual arts have the well-established National Association for the Visual Arts (NAVA) and Crafts

Australia; as well as a number of smaller organisations with specific interest in indigenous artists such as the Association of Northern, Kimberley and Arnhem Aboriginal Artists (AZNKAAA) and the Association of Central Australian Aboriginal Art and Crafts Centres—Desart.

Regional arts are represented by Regional Arts Australia. Several organisations specialise in legal and copyright matters, such as the Arts Law Centre of Australia and the Australian Copyright Council. Arts Industry Councils exist in States such as South Australia and Victoria as do co-ordinating bodies such as the Australian Performing Arts Centres Association. Representation for multicultural arts is provided in the Nexus Multicultural Arts Centre.

On a more industry-wide and employment level, leadership roles are played by the Media Entertainment and Arts Alliance (MEAA) the most significant arts union body; Live Performance Australia (the trading name of the Australian Entertainment Industry Association) and the recently revived National Arts and Cultural Alliance. The two latter bodies combine a variety of individual and corporate memberships. It has to be said that, with the possible exception of issues in the film and broadcasting industries, the role of the trade union movement in enhancing government support for the arts has been limited. Although there has been an understandable and proper concentration on matters of a primarily industrial nature and strenuous efforts to protect working conditions and interest of artists (such as by the provision of local content quotas) the union movement has not played a prominent role in the broader arts and cultural policy debate. It has certainly not been a significant source of financial support for various parts of the arts sector despite the efforts of companies such as the Melbourne Workers Theatre to bring arts activities into the workplace and make them more reflective of workplace-based concerns.[44]

There are two peak organisations in specific performing art-form sectors. Ausdance is the peak body in the dance industry with a national organisation constituted by seven State/territory members. The Australian Major Performing Arts Group (AMPAG) is an alliance of twenty-eight major performing arts companies crossing genres from opera and ballet, to music and theatre and circus.[45] A more recent arrival is Australia's BlakStage Alliance representing a number of Indigenous theatre companies.[46]

On a more informal level there is a Round Table group of Australia's major arts training institutions which includes NIDA, the Australian Film Television and Radio School (AFTRS), the National Institute of Circus Arts (NICA), the Australian Ballet School, the National Music School and the National Aboriginal Islanders Skills Development Association (NAISDA). Similarly, a number of the above organisations come together under the auspices of the Australia Council into a body called Artspeak.

On the financial side, the Australia Business Arts Foundation (AbaF) exists as a national organisation which promotes private sector support for the arts through programs of partnering, volunteering and promoting donations. It works to put arts organisations and business organisations into meaningful and mutually productive relationships, although it does not itself provide direct funding. AbaF has some 90 leading companies as members and is supported through the Cultural Development Program of the Federal Department of Environment, Water, Heritage and the Arts.

At what one might describe as a more intellectual level, there is the Canberra-based Council for the Humanities, Arts and Social Sciences (CHASS) which, while not an effective lobby group in itself, provides a useful platform for the exposition of policy ideas and debates.[47]

There is, however, no single national body which co-ordinates and represents the arts sector as a whole, and as such the sectoral interests of this vast constituency tend to focus upon matters of immediate interest to themselves, often at the cost of others.

Debates about funding for the arts often make comparison with funding for sport, and indeed it is not unusual for federal government portfolios to include both art and sport under the one Ministry. This was certainly the pattern with recent federal Coalition governments. Sport represents itself to the Federal Government through the Confederation of Australian Sport. This Confederation consists of the peak bodies in each of 30 sports—athletics, athletes with a disability, baseball, clay-target shooting, cricket, cycling, dancesport, equestrian, field archery, football, golf, gymnastics, international shooting, judo, kodokan, life-saving, masters athletics, masters swimming, netball, parachuting, powerlifting, rock n' roll dancesport, rugby league, ski and snowboard, sport knowledge, squash, surf life-saving, table tennis, touch football, university sport and volleyball. Although this is by no means a complete coverage of Australian sporting peak bodies (witness the absence of rugby union or AFL), it nevertheless covers an exceptionally wide and diverse field, overlapping Olympic sports with iconic areas such as surf life-saving.

The absence of major codes and disciplines does not, however, prevent these bodies from combining when common interests are at stake. For example, in May 2008 representatives of rugby league, rugby union, cricket, AFL, basketball and swimming combined to make a presentation to the Federal Government on the need for tax breaks or concessions to be provided to élite athletes.[48]

A similar diversity of membership is to be found in a body such as the Australian Council of Social Service (ACOSS). This body, which was established as far back as 1956, brings together all the State and Territory Councils of Social Service which themselves represent many thousand front-line community agencies and service providers. They also have as members the peak organisation of consumers and service providers, the major national religious and secular welfare agencies (e.g. Uniting Care, Anglicare, Catholic Welfare, Salvation Army and the Smith Family) and low-income groups (such as the Council for Single Mothers and the Pensioners organisations).

Bodies such as the CAS and ACOSS have established positions in relation to government decision-making which are crucial and central to their own interests and sectors, and governments, of whatever persuasion, would not contemplate making major policy decisions without some form of significant input from and consultation with these groups. It therefore seems surprising that given how the sports sector and the welfare sector have managed to create and sustain effective peak bodies operating across a vast diversity of constituent groups and interests that the arts community has not, at least not in the community of the theatre arts. There have been attempts to create and sustain such bodies, but the experiences of the Arts Alliance and CAPPA have hardly been encouraging.

8

Looking in the wrong place

Perhaps it is unfair to criticise, even indirectly, this lack of a national peak arts advocacy body—though the Australia Council may itself be regarded as an advocacy body *within* government. Perhaps it is time to recognise that the debate has moved on and the discussions about funding for the arts sector as such are becoming increasingly passé. In the first instance, it may be time to stop talking about the arts 'sector' and to talk about the arts 'stream'.

The term sector implies a degree of separation from the rest of social activity whether it be in relation to the arts as part of the cultural life of the nation, part of the economic life of the nation, part of the responsibility of governments across the nation or part of Australia's contribution to the common lot and heritage of humankind.

The term stream seems to me more genuinely representative of the role which the arts are playing increasingly across all levels of society. There is a heightened interest in the role the arts can play in relation to human health, environmental awareness, regional development, urban design and infrastructure, creativity and productivity in their broadest sense. And to their role in raising spiritual awareness, building a multicultural nation, promoting reconciliation between races, interpreting our national history and our national myths, and enhancing the understanding of science. A recent Sydney exhibition sponsored by the *New Scientist* magazine featured a selection of the most outstanding photographs that presented images of science in a way which helped the public to understand. The photographs were pure art and the subject pure science.

The arts themselves are becoming increasingly understood as part of growing recognition of a 'creative sector' being part of the Australian economy and national life. In this respect, the work of Richard Florida has been increasingly influential. In his seminal work, *The Rise of the Creative Class*, he opened a discussion of what he called the 'creative sector' of the United States economy, in which he claimed that

> [t]he wealth generated by the creative sector is astounding: It accounts for nearly half all wage and salary income in the United States, $ 1.7 trillion dollars, as much as the manufacturing and service sectors combined.[49]

Turning Disraeli's aphorism of two nations on its head, Florida asserts that the United States is splitting into 'two separate and distinct nations, economically, culturally and politically'. For Florida, the division is between those parts of the United States locked in traditional styles of life and thinking in places based upon 'older-style industries and slow growth', and those living in a more 'secular, cosmopolitan and wealthy' environment based upon emerging new, hi-tech and fast-growing industries. The inhabitants of the former are, he says, increasingly angry and the inhabitants of the latter increasingly seen as hedonistic, shallow and self-absorbed. To restore homogeneity, the challenge faced by those who are part of his 'creative class' (although they may not recognise this themselves) is to ensure that those who are not part of this class are not entirely left behind. In his view they need either to be brought into the tent or at least be made partial beneficiaries of it. Above all, Florida makes the points that 'creativity [...] is now the *decisive* source of competitive advantage'; that 'creativity has come to be the most highly prized commodity in our economy' and that 'the creative individual is no longer viewed as an iconoclast. He—or she—is the new mainstream'.[50]

In the wake of Florida's work, attempts have been made to link the ideas of 'creative arts' with the 'creative economy' and to trace the roots of both back to the concept of civic humanism in the 1700s.[51] Efforts have been made to give precise definition to what might or might not be included in the term 'creative industries', if for no other reason than to measure their output and value.[52]

Initiatives promoting the value of the creative sector can take place at almost any level. The City of New York invests massively in the development and promotion of its arts industry. Its Department of Cultural Affairs has an annual budget in excess of $130 million.[53] On a smaller scale, the recent launch of the Sustainable Sydney 2030 Plan by Lord Mayor Clover Moore accords a significant place to the promotion of the creative arts as central to plans for urban renewal.[54]

This is not the place to take that debate further, other than to note that creativity has well and truly arrived in Australia. Central to the whole 2020 Summit initiative of the Rudd Government was the integration of discussion about the arts, film and design into a broader discussion about Australia as a 'creative nation' ending with a policy recommendation to 'double cultural output' and recognise the centrality of the arts in the promotion of creativity. In May 2008, Arts Minister Peter Garrett's media release in association with the first Federal Budget, described the arts-support measures in the Budget as 'New Initiatives for a Creative Australia', although in truth they were quite plainly a series of support measures for individual artists and performing arts companies.[55]

It seems to me now that the rhetoric is getting somewhat confused and opaque. The slippery segues from art to culture to creativity, from creativity to output to productivity leave one in real danger of missing what the debate is all about. The looseness of terms and definitions, the inexactness of measurements and the incomprehensibility of some of the jargon becomes mind-numbing. If this is the vision of the future, if the arts are to be subsumed into a broader and hopefully deeper debate about creativity, then many of the old paradigms will have to be replaced. Such is the fate of paradigms in any case.

This new 'concordat' for the arts, as one British commentator has put it, assumes major changes will take place on both sides of the debate, both among the politicians and among the arts community.[56] My own experiences have given me too great a familiarity with the old paradigm. It was constructed on the basis of mutual suspicion.

No one has written more thoughtfully on this disconnect between the politicians, the arts professionals and the public than John Holden who, in two brilliant essays published by the British think-tank Demos,[57] has sought to develop a new paradigm for discourse about arts funding and policy.

He writes:

> Politics has struggled to understand culture and failed to engage with it effectively. Cultural professionals have focused on satisfying the policy demands of their funders in an attempt to gain the same unquestioning support for culture that exists for health or education; but the truth is that politicians will never be able to give that support until there exists a more broadly based and better articulated democratic consensus.

And later,

> Politicians and policymakers appear to care most about instrumental economic and social outcomes, but the public and most professionals have a completely different set of concerns. As a result the relationships between the public, politicians and professionals have become dysfunctional. The 'cultural system' has become a closed and ill-tempered conversation between professionals and politicians, while the news pages of the media play a destructive role between politics and the public.

His solution is for arts professionals to invest more time and effort in establishing their 'democratic credentials'. That is, to engage with the public and engender public support for what they are doing or seeking to do and to understand that politicians will basically fund those things for which they believe there is public support.

Holden again:

> The problems are clearly systemic but the solutions must start with cultural professionals. Their opportunity is that the value of culture to the public is unlimited and infinitely expandable. The challenge, which is already being taken up in some places, is to create a different alignment between culture, politics and the public. In practice this will require courage, confidence and radicalism on the part of professionals in finding new ways to build greater legitimacy directly with citizens. The evidence so far suggests that such an approach would be successful and would serve the aims of all concerned—politicians, the professionals themselves, and above all the public.[58]

This is in no sense to imply that the arts have to 'dumb down' their arguments or that the task which they face is Herculean. Far from it. Almost all surveys of public opinion in Australia demonstrate a high level of public support for the arts and for the provision of funds to arts and cultural activities and institutions. Australians engage widely with a vast variety of arts activities from the purchase of DVDs and CDs, to attendance at the cinema, theatres, music festivals and concerts, art galleries, museums, circus, children's theatre and free performances.

In 2000, the Australia Council commissioned Saatchi and Saatchi to undertake a major investigation of the attitude of Australians towards the arts. In both their report to the Council and in a major volume published separately, the consultants noted the high level of support shown by the general public for the arts. Interestingly, one of their principal conclusions eerily anticipates the conclusions of John Holden:

> Nevertheless while some Australians love the arts, others don't feel so positive about them. On the one hand, some members of the public hold out-of-date perceptions of what constitute 'the arts' and what the arts can mean to them personally and nationally. On the other hand, some people in the arts sector apparently hold out-of-date perceptions of who constitutes the Australian public, what motivates them and how to deal with them. This could be a classic case of mistaken identity. However, if the arts sector wants to promote the value of the arts to all Australians, every member of that sector needs to take the responsibility for any gap in these

> perceptions. The sector needs to improve its own understanding of the Australian public and it needs actively to work to change perceptions of the arts among that public.[59]

This is a long way from the nature of arts advocacy strategies outlined two decades ago in Tim Rowse's well-known study, *Arguing the Arts.*[60] But it could be argued still that far too many Australian arts practitioners and professionals are stuck in a time warp twenty years old.

Not that private sector money or financial support is lacking either. In May 2008 a report from AbaF disclosed that arts companies had attracted $171.1 million in sponsorship from business and donations in the preceding financial year.[61] Australia has been slower than the United Kingdom to pick up on the consequences of this debate and redefinition. Sir Brian McMaster's 2007 review of arts funding in the United Kingdom focuses upon arts funding arrangements within a world where 'creativity' is the touchstone, while proposing a far greater direct role for the funding authorities in the appointment processes of the organisations they fund.[62] By contrast, the most recent contribution to the debate in Australia, a recent Platform Paper by Cathy Hunt and Phyllida Shaw, surveying past models of arts funding and showing why most of them failed, then went on to propose what they characterise as an holistic approach away from the old paradigms and emphasising partnership and sustainability. However, to my mind, a close reading of their arguments and proposals reveals essentially nothing new or challenging and indeed has all the aspects of yet another rearrangement of the *Titanic* deckchairs.[63]

On a more positive note, the launch of *Australia's Performing Arts: We All Play a Part*— billed as a campaign not just about funding, but to show how the cultural sector can 'contribute to the economy and promote social cohesion'[64] and where the aim was to raise the profile of the arts industry—may be a positive sign that the paradigm shift has commenced, at least in some quarters.

I hope this is not asking too much. Let me quote Holden again:

> Politics finds culture difficult in other ways as well. Politics is concerned with mass social outcomes: it is about simplification and decision-making on a large scale. Art by contrast is about the individual, about complexity and subtlety. The former director of the National Theatre, Sir Richard Eyre, has pointed out that there is a fundamental incompatibility between politics and the arts. He quotes the American writer Philip Roth as saying: *Politics is the great generaliser and literature the great particulariser, and not only are they in an inverse relationship to each other, they are in an antagonistic relationship. How can you be an artist and renounce the nuance? How can you be a politician and allow the nuance?*[65] There is a huge disconnect between the public's idea of culture and what it is for, and the way that politics and policy talk about it.[66]

Even if it is asking a lot, it is still worth doing.

Perhaps there can be an intermediate or starting-point in this attempt to shift the paradigm.

The previous Coalition Government introduced a program in 1991 to establish Co-operative Research Centres across Australia to bring together researchers of special expertise and interest in areas identified as being of genuine national significance but not well enough catered for in traditional funding models. The objective of the Centres was 'to enhance Australia's industrial, commercial and economic growth through the development of sustained, user-driven, cooperative public-private research centres that achieve high levels of outcomes in adoption and commercialisation'. To date 58 such centres have been funded across six sectors including that of information technology and communications. Perhaps what we need is a CRC in Arts Policy and Research. The new Labor Government has announced a review of aspects of the national innovation system[67] and there is no reason why innovation in the arts and cultural sector should be excluded from this review. Perhaps the indication that the Rudd Government is to fund a Creative Industries Innovation Centre, which may extend its largesse to small-to-medium-sized Australian arts companies, is a positive straw in the wind.[68] I will be interested to see which, if any, of the arts advocacy bodies has made submissions to the current Review.[69]

After all, if we have a CRC in Australian Weed Management, perhaps one that looks at the health and future of the garden would not go astray.

9

Doing it right—doing it not so right

It may be useful to reflect upon two recent and significant events that took place within the arts industry and brought a close interaction between the wishes of the arts sector and the higher reaches of the political game. In doing so, I suggest one course of action which was based upon what I have described as the old paradigm and one which was based upon the new. The fact that I characterise the former as one of great success and the other as a source of disappointment only goes to show how hard the desired transition from one to the other will actually be.

Freeing the Archive

In 1935 the Commonwealth established a National Historic Film and Speaking Record Library which was located within the National Library of Australia. In 1984 the National Film and Sound Archive (NFSA) was separated and given its own status as an independent agency within the then Department of Home Affairs and the Environment. In April 1984 Labor Arts Minister Cohen announced in Parliament that the NFSA would be established as an independent statutory authority; and in October 1985 the Advisory Committee appointed by the Minister delivered its report,[70] a blueprint for the future of the new independent institution. However, despite the promise, the NFSA legislation never saw the light of day and the Archive remained an agency within the relevant (arts) department.

In 2002/3 the Coalition Government instituted a review of collecting institutions which, to the surprise of everyone concerned, resulted in the NFSA being placed within a restricted Australian Film Commission (AFC) from July 2003. This arrangement turned out to be disastrous. The interests of the AFC and the NFSA were never at one; their aims, objectives, philosophies and cultures were incompatible. This mismatch was brought into sharp focus when the AFC produced a discussion paper, *Stage 2 Directions,* in December 2003 which in effect provided for the dismantlement of the Archive's core functions and the replacement or transfer of its key personnel.

The normally quiescent archive and historical community reacted with dismay and anger. Their protests were co-ordinated by the Friends of the Archives support group and a new group which had come into existence in May 2003 to agitate against the continued submergence of the NFSA within the AFC. This was the Archive Forum, comprised of figures in the film, archive, historical and political communities, including this author. Reaction to the AFC proposals led to some 140 submissions being made to the AFC and to leading political figures both in government and in opposition, particularly the then Labor Shadow Arts Minister, Senator Kate Lundy, and her ACT Liberal colleague Senator Garry Humphries. A series of public consultations on the AFC proposals revealed widespread hostility to the proposals; resolutions of opposition to them were passed by the Australian Society of Archivists[71] and the Australian Historical Society. There was even a physical demonstration against the proposals at the Archive. The Archive Forum produced a major and damning report on the AFC proposals which received wide circulation.[72] In co-operation with Labor and other Opposition parliamentarians the issues of the future of the NFSA were raised regularly at hearings of the Senate Estimates Committees and through a series of parliamentary questions. In addition the arts writers of the *Canberra Times* were briefed on a regular basis and several feature articles appeared, the tone of which were hostile to the AFC's proposals.[73] The reaction of the AFC, forced into a backdown on its original *Directions* proposals, was so aggressive and hostile that the Archive Forum determined to renew its push for full statutory independence for the NFSA.

The Coalition Government accepted that the AFC *Directions* blueprint was not viable but was not prepared to accede to demands for statutory independence for the NFSA. It should be recorded, however, that Senator Garry identified himself as a public supporter of NFSA independence. As a result proponents turned to the Opposition and persuaded the Labor Party to give a commitment in its 2007 federal election policy to provide for this.

The election of the Rudd Government in November 2007 led in remarkably short order to the passage of the *National Film and Sound Archive Act* in March 2008. Although Arts Minister Kemp had opposed such a move, the new Shadow Minister for the Arts, Dr Sharman Stone, was persuaded by members of the Archive Forum to support the legislation and it passed the Senate where the Coalition parties still held an absolute majority. Not only was the legislation passed with bipartisan support, but Arts Minister Garrett subsequently appointed the chair of the Archive Forum (who happens to be the author) as the inaugural chair of the new Board of the Archive. In addition the Deputy Chair of the Archive Forum and two other activists were appointed to the seven-person Board.

This was an exercise in old-fashioned politics. A determined group of well-informed and dedicated individuals embarked on a campaign to reverse a significant government policy in the arts. By the traditional methods of lobbying the Opposition, seeking support within the Government's own ranks, mobilising external support groups and interests, using the parliamentary meetings such as estimates committees to raise questions and concerns, and planting or encouraging favourable media reporting, this complete reversal of policy was achieved. What is more, the poachers were then appointed as the gamekeepers and of course, now have to deliver on the claims they made about the benefits of their preferred course of action.

The 2020 Summit

If ever there was going to be a time and an opportunity to put the arts centre stage and to provoke serious public debate about arts policy, arts funding and the centrality (or otherwise) of the arts in Australian public life, the 2020 Summit should have been the opportunity. In my assessment it failed to do so, and although its proponents argue (with some justification) that one must wait for the Government's promised response before making final judgement, it is still to me an opportunity missed.

The whole idea of the 2020 exercise was to bring together the best and the brightest, to let them talk, to develop ideas, to articulate visions and to present them within the wider framework of the remaking of our national life. At least that was the plan and the promise.

The participants in the 'Towards a Creative Australia' panel, chaired by Cate Blanchett, Professor Julianne Schultz and Arts Minister Peter Garrett, brought together a fascinating cross-section of the whole arts community. It ranged from the most powerful establishment figures (David Gonski, Roger Wilkins, Rupert Myer, Saul Eslake) through a range of practitioners, writers and artists to the young tyros of contemporary Australian theatre (Matt Lutton, Nicholas Marchand, Marion Potts). Notably, regrettably absent was any significant representation from arts educators or the major national theatre schools. Both these sectors provided a raft of self-nominees none of whom was chosen and this exclusion of the formal arts training institutions input represents a critical failure to understand the integrated nature of the arts industry.

Despite this, instead of there being a genuine free-flow of ideas, it is apparent that the Summit sessions quickly degenerated into 'facilitator directed' modules and that there was no serious time available for debate or exposition of ideas. Participants complained that they were assigned to subcommittee sessions in which they had no particular interest or expertise; that they were herded into agreement with a pre-planned agenda of the Government's determination; and that both facilitators and chairpersons filtered out unpalatable ideas in order to produce anodyne conclusions.[74] It is regrettable that the Creative Australia sessions were not open to the media,[75] so it is hard to make clear assessments of what input was made by delegates and what was filtered into the final communiqué.

The 'big ideas' put forward—though they were not terribly 'big', really—included:

- A proposal for 'practitioners in residence' to be introduced into our schools. It is interesting that this 'Summit idea' came in fact a few days *after* Arts Minister Garrett announced that he would be raising it at the meeting.[76] Any consideration of the practicality of this proposal and the likelihood that the better-resourced schools would benefit most, appeared not to have been canvassed.
- A proposal to digitise the collections of the major national institutions (undefined) by 2020—a project that in most cases is already well under way.
- A proposal to 'make creativity a national research priority with funding access to R&D, ARC and similar funding'. Creative research, of course, is already funded and the recommendation is not accompanied with any support for increased R&D or ARC funding *per se*—so presumably this new 'priority' area is to compete with already present priorities.

- A proposal to create a 'National Endowment Fund for the Arts': perhaps modelled on the Coalition Government's original Future Fund but having parallels with the United States National Endowment for the Arts. However the American model operates in a different milieu from Australia, as evidenced by its Chairperson's Address to the United States National Commission for UNESCO Annual Conference in 2005,[77] and has more in common with the long-abandoned Challenge Grants Scheme of thirty years ago.
- A proposal to fund creative endeavours 'through a 1% creative dividend from all government departments for expenditure on the arts'. This merely repeats a long established UNESCO objective of 1% of government expenditure on the arts.[78] On the other hand, this dividend is to be made on top of the 2% 'efficiency dividend' imposed on departments and agencies in the May 2008 Budget—an imposition which has already led to staff retrenchments and program cancellations in major national arts institutions.[79] An imposition like this implies that asking the Department of Health to divert 1% into arts expenditure is a better use of its money than building hospitals, researching cancer cures or tackling the tragedy of Indigenous health disadvantage.

One could hardly cavil with some of the other ideas such as revisions of the taxation system, adopting a whole-of-government approach,[80] recognising the centrality of Indigenous arts and culture and the improvement of the position of arts education in the national schools agenda. *However, not one of these ideas could be said to be original, let alone radical.* The centrality of arts education in schools was the centrepiece of the then UNESCO Director-General's (Frederico Mayor) address at the General Conference of 1999. Perhaps the only radical idea put forward at the Summit was the reinstatement of death duties—a sure-fire policy to enhance public support for the arts.

What I found disappointing was the essentially conservative nature of the ideas advanced when clearly a new government and a new process were offering the opportunities to really think outside the traditional squares and the established paradigms. The paradigm shift in government was not matched by any paradigm shift in conceptual analysis or thinking.

Again, I appreciate the very fact that the Summit took place was significant, that much useful and accessible preparatory work was done (and is available online) and that post-Summit chat-rooms and discussions groups have developed. Perhaps like all (even ex-) politicians I am too outcomes-focussed and do not give enough credit to process, innovation and development. But, as they say, the proof of the pudding will be in the eating.

More disappointingly, however, a close reading of the Summit report reveals a deafening silence on the role of the arts as a significant tool in Australian's international diplomacy—'soft power', to use the approved jargon. Other small (power) countries such as Denmark, Finland or Egypt have made cultural diplomacy a central feature of their international activities, not just leaving this field to the giants like Russia, China, France, Britain or the United States.[81] Not a word in the open public discourse from our Creative Australia summiteers on this front, perhaps not surprisingly, given that the very first arts funding decision made by the Rudd Government was to axe the $20.4 million program (*Australia on the World Stage*) which was managed through the Department of Foreign Affairs and Trade to improve market access for Australian cultural exports.[82]

At the end of the day, what the Creative Australia session really urged was to 'double cultural output'. What this actually means remains either undefined, or, in Humpty-Dumpty fashion, whatever each individual says it means. However, the accompanying statement proclaimed that: '*To achieve this there is a need to implement policies that will produce a sustainable creative sector and support artists, build educational capacity, integrate indigenous and settler perspectives and recognise the centrality of the arts and creativity to the whole economy.*' I for one do not understand what that means either practically or even aspirationally, but I do recognise that when appealing to the wider Australian community for support (and money) describing them as 'settlers' is not a good way to start!

10

Advocates and acolytes

There is a final word of warning here. It is, I believe, highly undesirable for any group in the community, especially if they represent an on-going interest, to become too closely associated with any single political party. No matter how attractive that appears when the party concerned is in government, the political wheel always turns. As an arts advocate there would be few Australians better placed than Oscar winner and *über*-mum Cate Blanchett. She, together with Julianne Schultz was one of the co-chairs of the Creative Australia stream at the 2020 summit. This followed her well-publicised appearances at the side of (now) Arts Minister Peter Garrett throughout the election campaign and at his victory party. If this much-publicised endorsement continues, Ms Blanchett's capacity to influence any future Coalition Government is likely to be discounted, her views dismissed as those of a mere 'partisan'.[83] The Coalition parties still hold a powerful position in the Senate, potentially capable of frustrating government plans and legislation. The building of a bipartisan consensus in support of the arts is vital for their future growth and well-being.

This is the fundamental dilemma for arts advocates. They need to maintain credibility across the political divide. They need to be able to open doors on both sides of the aisle and to have influence across both sides of the Chambers. Indeed, these days across all sides: Labor, Coalition, Green, Family First, No-Pokies, independents.

Unlike the world of science where public figures such as Sir Gustav Nossal, Nobel Laureate Peter Doherty, Professors Fiona Stanley, David Pennington, Ian Guss, John Dwyer or even ex-politicians such as Professor Peter Baume are never thought of in terms of their personal politics, *most artists are tagged as politically partisan and this weakens their abilities to be truly effective.* It's a hard call to ask people who parade the passionate side of their nature to be dispassionate, but it's a requirement to do the job and the dangers are great of falling into the trap of becoming a victim of what Marcuse calls 'repressive tolerance': 'the passive toleration of entrenched and established attitudes and ideas even if their damaging effect on man and nature is evident'. This way the system simply co-opts its critics as part of the system, embraces them personally and ignores their ideas and criticisms.

The Australian political system is one of the most remarkably open in the world, and Australian politicians and decision makers among the most accessible. However, a mere continuation of the tired rhetoric that it's all about money and there's never enough of it will get the creative and performing arts nowhere. The brave new worlds of Richard Florida and John Holden are becoming nascent voices in the emerging

Australian debate about creativity. With luck and a great deal more work and cooperation, perhaps the lessons of the past will be learnt and the arts begin to take a new, creative direction.

Getting heard is not difficult—having something to say is much more of a challenge.

Endnotes

1 'Picasso painting breaks Australian art sale record', *Reuters News Service*, 18 June 2008.
2 Valerie Lawson, 'Ballet's wild colonial stings from the grave', *Sydney Morning Herald*, 18 June 2008.
3 *Does Australia Need a Cultural Policy?*, Platform Paper No. 7 (Sydney: Currency House, 2006), pp. 32–3.
4 Between 1980 and 1996 some 65 recipients of these fellowships were paid a total of $11.7million, with some artists receiving up to $219,000 over a three-year period.
5 See, for example, Wayne Harrison's 1994 lecture, 'The Civil War and How to End it', in *The Parsons Lectures: The Philip Parsons Memorial Lectures on the Performing Arts,1993–2003*, ed. by Katharine Brisbane (Sydney: Currency House, 2003), pp. 19–41.
6 Department of Communications and the Arts, *Creative Nation* (Canberra, October 1994) p. 7.
7 'The Politics of Creativity', *Arts Monthly*, 1 November 1994, p. 10.
8 'Written into the vision splendid', *Sydney Morning Herald*, 7 March 2005.
9 Ibid.
10 European Australia's first arts subsidy appears to have been as far back as 1818–19, when poet Michael Massey Robinson was granted two cows from the government herd 'for his services as Poet Laureate'. See Throsby, p. 5.

11 J. A. La Nauze, *Alfred Deakin: A Biography* (Hong Kong: Angus & Robertson, 1979), pp. 430–1. The scheme was not without its critics, one Labor member remarking that it was unnecessary, since 'those who lead sober and decent lives are very well paid' (quoted by John Rickard, *H.B. Higgins: The Rebel as Judge* (Sydney: Allen & Unwin, 1984), p. 165).

12 The value of the fund, its success in assisting the publication of some 234 books, its support of literary magazines such as *Meanjin, Southerly, Quadrant, Overland* etc. and its assistance to almost every Australian writer and poet of note is documented in Justin Macdonnell, *Arts, Minister?* (Sydney: Currency Press, 1992), pp. 10–11.

13 Parliamentary Research Service, *Arts Policy in Australia: A History of Commonwealth Involvement in the Arts*, Background Paper No. 5, Commonwealth Parliamentary Library, Canberra, 1994.

14 The Government contributed $60,000 and a further $180,000 was raised by public subscription. Prior to the establishment of the Australian Council for the Arts, this Trust was the principal arts funding body in Australia.

15 Macdonnell, pp. 15–19.

16 This provided for a 150–per cent write-off of film investment expenditure in the year of expenditure. However, it did not require that the film, once made, ever actually be released commercially!

17 Macdonnell, p. 232.

18 At the time I myself was Chairman of the Government Parties Environment and Arts Backbench Committee, which was required to give its agreement to the Minister's plans for the film industry incentives scheme and so had a significant part in its introduction. At no stage was I lobbied in support of the plan

other than by producer organisations. No individual artists or film stars ever sought to make contact.

19 *Arts, Minister?*, p. 232.

20 Michael Bodey, 'Disquiet on the offset', *Weekend Australian*, 10–11 May 2008. This emphasises the extent to which the Australian film industry 'sells' itself internationally primarily on the generous financial incentives provided for filmmaking in Australia.

21 Luke Slattery, 'Work in progress', *Weekend Australian*, 21–2 June 2008, *Review*, p. 4.

22 Stephen Bevis, 'It's time to mine creative riches in boom landscape', *West Australian*, 14 June 2008.

23 Jennifer Craik, *Re-visioning Arts and Cultural Policy: Current Impasses and Future Directions* (Canberra: ANU E-Press, 2007).

24 K. S. Inglis, *This is the ABC: The Australian Broadcasting Commission, 1932–1983* (Melbourne: Melbourne University Press, 1983).

25 The only subsequent mention of this report was a commitment to enact those of its recommendations compatible with the Coalition Parties' Ethnic Affairs Policy in the Liberal and National Parties Arts *Policy Document: The Excitement of the Arts* (1988).

26 Australia Council, *Annual Report, 1978/9*, p. 4.

27 Part of this dissatisfaction resulted from the combination of the across-the-board funding cuts of the Fraser 'Razor Gang' and the introduction of the Community Arts Board into the Australia Council as a further potential competitor for funds.

28 In 1985, the Australian Ballet, Australian Opera and two AETT orchestras absorbed one quarter of all Australia Council funds allocated. Apart from 'ceiling' funding, there was also a suggestion of 'plateau' funding, which sought merely to keep companies 'stable' in their level of support without any allowance for real

growth opportunities. The Theatre Board's approach (known as the Rotherwood Plan) also commenced a process of dividing companies into three distinct categories—national and state companies; innovative, alternative or regional companies; and single project activities—and of seeking to assess and fund each on the basis of different criteria.

29 See Macdonnell, chap. 8.

30 McLeay Report, Recommendation 17. See Barry Cohen's response in the House of Representatives, *Hansard*, 28 May 1987.

31 Working Party of Cultural Ministers Council Standing Committee, *Report to Ministers on Examination of the Small-to-Medium Performing Arts Sector* (March 2002).

32 Karen van Ulzen, 'Disaster or Opportunity?', *Dance Australia* (December 2006–January 2007), pp. 29–30. Corrie Perkin, 'Steps in time', *Weekend Australian*, 26–7 July 2008.

33 For an interesting perspective on this debate in the United Kingdom, particularly in Wales, see Geraint Tlafan Davies, *At Arm's Length: Recollections and Reflections on the Arts, Media and a Young Democracy* (Bridgend, Wales: Seren, 2008). For some interesting historical background to the UK debate, see Robert Hutchison, *The Politics of the Arts Council* (London: Sinclair Browne, 1982), pp. 16–17.

34 Australian Labor Party, *New Directions for the Arts: Supporting a Vibrant and Diverse Australian Arts Sector* (September 2007).

35 See Macdonnell, pp. 370–6.

36 Actors Equity and the Musicians Union subsequently merged into membership of the Media Entertainment and Arts Alliance.

37 CAPPA was another short-lived peak lobby group, coming into existence in late 1979 and dwindling in

the mid-1980s. Interestingly, its first chairperson was Tony Staley, a former Minister for the Arts in the Fraser Government and yet another person of great political influence with the government of the day.

38 Sue Beale, 'Industry Comments', in *Shooting the Pianist: The Role of Government in the Arts*, ed. by Philip Parsons (Sydney: Currency Press, 1987), p. 102.

39 Jennifer Radbourne, 'Commonwealth Arts Administration: an Historical Perspective 1945–1990' (Unpublished PhD thesis, University of Queensland Department of History, 1992) p. 255.

40 *Commonwealth Arts Administration*, p. viii.

41 *Re-visioning Arts and Cultural Policy*, p. 19.

42 Katrina Strickland, 'Review-based cycle winds up', *Australian*, 27 December 2004.

43 David Throsby and Devon Mills, *When are You Going to Get a Real Job?: An Economic Study of Australian Artists* (Sydney: ARC Report, 1989) and David Throsby and Virginia Hollister, *Don't give up your day job: an economic study of professional artists in Australia* (Australia Council for the Arts, Sydney, 2003).

44 See Glenn D'Cruz, *Class Act: Melbourne Workers Theatre, 1987–2007* (Carlton, Vic.: Vulgar Press, 2007), which makes clear how little financial support has been forthcoming from Union sources.

45 Membership of the Australian Major Performing Arts Group comprises the Adelaide Symphony Orchestra, Australian Brandenberg Orchestra, Australian Chamber Orchestra, Bangarra Dance Theatre, Bell Shakespeare Company, Black Swan Theatre Company, Circus Oz, Company B Belvoir Street Theatre, Malthouse Theatre, Melbourne Symphony Orchestra, Melbourne Theatre Company, Musica Viva, Opera Australia, State Opera of South Australia, State Theatre Company of South Australia, Sydney Dance Company, Sydney

Symphony Orchestra, Sydney Theatre Company, Tasmanian Symphony Orchestra, The Australian Ballet, Queensland Orchestra, West Australian Ballet, West Australian Opera and West Australian Symphony Orchestra.

46 Membership includes Baru Kadal, Ilbijerri, Kooemba Jdarra, Kurruru, Moogahlin Theatre, Yirra Yaakin

47 See, for example, (then) Arts Minister Brandis welcome speech to the CHASS Conference on 20 June 2007, used by the Minister to set out the broad shape of the Government's approach to 'cultural policy'.

48 ABC Radio National, *Breakfast*, 1 May 2008.

49 *The Rise of the Creative Class*, rev. edn (New York: Basic Books, 2004), p. xiv.

50 *The Rise of the Creative Class*, pp. 5–6.

51 John Hartley, 'Creative Industries', in *Creative Industries*, ed. by John Hartley (London: Blackwell, 2005), p. 6.

52 The Work Foundation: *Staying Ahead: The Economic Performance of the UK's Creative Industries* (UK Government, London, June 2007).

53 Richard Lacayo, 'Culture Club', *Time*, 28 January 2008, p. 42.

54 City of Sydney, 'Sustainable Sydney 2030: City of Sydney Strategic Plan', Final Consultation Draft (2008), Section 7.

55 'New initiatives for a creative Australia', Media Release, 13 May 2008.

56 John Tusa, *Engaged with the Arts: Writings from the Frontline* (London: Tauris, 2007), p. 55.

57 *Cultural Value and the Crisis of Legitimacy: Why Culture Needs a Democratic Mandate* (London: Demos, 2006) and *Capturing Cultural Value: How Culture has Become a Tool of Government Policy* (London: Demos, 2004).

58 Ibid.

59 Saatchi and Saatchi (Paul Costantoura), *Australians and*

the Arts (Sydney: Federation Press, 2001), p. vii.

60 (Ringwood, Vic.: Penguin, 1985).

61 Matthew Westwood, 'Business hands out a cool $171million in gifts', *Australian*, 15 May 2008.

62 Sir Brian McMaster, *Supporting Excellence in the Arts* (Department for Culture, Media and Sport, London, January 2008), p. 13.

63 *A Sustainable Arts Sector: What Will it Take?*, Platform Paper No. 15 (Sydney: Currency House, 2008).

64 Matthew Westwood, 'Arts sector plays new tune', *Australian*, 3 April 2008.

65 Richard Eyre, 'Ballot-box blues', *Guardian*, 26 March 2005.

66 Holden, *Capturing Cultural Value*, pp. 28–9.

67 Senator Hon Kim Carr, 'Government announces Review of National Innovation System', Media Release, 22 January 2008. The Review Panel is headed by Dr Terry Cutler, Chair of the Advisory Board for the Centre of Excellence for Creative Industries, and includes Professor Glyn Davis who co-chaired the co-ordinating committee for the 2020 Summit.

68 Rosemary Sorensen, 'Professor explores innovative angles for funding', *Australian*, 31 March 2008.

69 'Not so many thought-provoking, pushing-the-boundaries submissions as I would like,' was Dr Cutler's verdict. He was speaking at a Currency House breakfast at the Sydney Opera House on 19 August 2008.

70 National Film and Sound Archive Advisory Committee (Joan Long, Chair), *Time in Our Hands* (Canberra, 1985).

71 Australian Society of Archivists, 'Archivists plea for independence', Press Release, 22 September 2004 and 'Archivists want action on National Film and Sound Archive', Press Release, 20 September 2004.

72 See 'Cinderella Betrayed: The Show Won't Fit' (Archive Forum, 20 January 2004), available at www.afiresearch.rmit.edu.au/archiveforum (accessed 31 July 2008).

73 See Helen Musa, 'Relief but apprehension at National Film and Sound Archive over Dalton's move', *Canberra Times*, 14 January 2006 and 'Lobbyists call for independent Film and Sound Archive, *Canberra Times*, 15 July 2006. Also Lynden Barber, 'Row heats up over Film and Sound Archive', *Australian*, 11 February 2004.

74 See, for example, Bob Ellis, '2020 vision obscured by spin', *Encore* (May 2008), pp. 8–9. On the use of the Summit as providing 'some legitimisation for a pre-existing idea', see Judith Brett, 'The Nation Reviewed', *The Monthly*, June 2008, pp. 10–11. Also Imre Salusinsky, 'Labor agenda "foisted onto summiteers"', *Australian*, 26–27 April 2008; Jewel Topsfield and Peter Ker, '2020 bagged by unhappy summiteers', *Age*, 24 April 2008. On 22 April, the *Age* also published a piece by summiteer Julian Meyrick, 'No easy answers, but talking opens up new opportunities', which, although a more balanced and positive analysis, is not uncritical.

75 Unlike the sessions on national security (featuring Victoria's Chief Police Commissioner Christine Nixon, Defence Chief Angus Houston and AFP Commissioner Mick Keelty) which were open to the public.

76 '"Ageing artists should teach", says Garrett', *West Australian*, 18 April 2008.

77 Dana Gioia (Chairman, National Endowment for the Arts), 'A View of Culture and the Arts', Opening Plenary Address US National Commission for UNESCO Annual Conference, 6 June 2005, U.S. Department of State, available at www.state.gov./p/io/unesdco/51700.htm (accessed 31 July 2008).

78 Such a policy was implemented by President Mitterrand of France and advocated by Sir Claus Moser in his address, 'Paying for the arts: patrons, politicians and the public', published as a *Conversazione* arising from the Seminar on the Sociology of Culture at La Trobe University, 1984.

79 The impact of such efficiency dividends, with special reference to whether or not they may have 'a disproportionate impact on smaller agencies' (which includes all the arts/cultural agencies), is to be examined by the Parliamentary Joint Committee on Public Accounts and Audit. Submissions detailing this impact are available at http://www.aph.gov.au/house/committee/jpaa/efficdiv/subs.htm (accessed 1 August 2008). For a particular example, see Phillip Hudson, 'Rudd's axe could sink museum fleet', *Sydney Morning Herald*, 2–3 August 2008. It might also be noted that the previous Coalition Government exempted (by way of additional supplementation) all the arts agencies and the Australia Council from the payment of any such efficiency dividends.

80 This is hardly a new idea. Indeed, the first Annual Report of the Australia Council (January-December 1973, p. 13) asserted that 'the arts are increasingly seen as relevant to social welfare, urban planning, regional development, recreation, immigration, tourism, education, international relations, local government, management policies and welfare programmes in industry and in trade unions'. Today one could add health, where a specialist journal, *Arts+Medicine*, is published as a 'Creative Health Magazine for Doctors'.

81 In some respects the United States has led in this area with the Nixon Administration's use of 'ping-pong' diplomacy to open up dialogue with China and the

February 2008 visit of the New York Philharmonic to North Korea.

82 A clear appreciation of the role of 'soft diplomacy' is evident in the Lowy Institute's Policy Brief, *Football Diplomacy* (written by Anthony Bubalo), which provides a stunning analysis and program for using Australia's emerging role as a soccer nation to enhance our influence, trade and diplomacy in the Asian region.

83 This symbiotic relationship climaxed with *Time*'s request that Blanchett write a colour piece on Kevin Rudd for the 12 May 2008 issue featuring the year's 100 most influential figures. She shared duties with Henry Kissinger writing about Hu Jintao, Bill Clinton on Tony Blair, Laura Bush on Khaled Hosseini and Desmond Tutu on Peter Gabriel.

Appendix

Public Inquiries into the Arts

Broadcasting

- Royal Commission on Wireless (the Hammond) 1928
- The Parliamentary Standing Committee on Broadcasting 1946/7
- Committee of Review of the ABC (Fitzgerald) 1947
- Report on the Structure of the Australian Broadcasting System and Associated Matters (Green) 1976

Film and television

- Royal Commission on the Moving Picture Industry in Australia (Marks) 1928
- Royal Commission on Performing Rights (Owen) 1932/3
- Royal Commission on Television (Paton) 1954
- Senate Select Committee on the Encouragement of Australian Production for Television (Vincent) 1964
- Review of the Australian Film Industry (Gonski) 1997.

Other

- National Art Gallery Committee of Inquiry (Lindsay) 1966
- Committee of Inquiry into Museums and National Collections (Piggott) 1974

- Report of the Committee of Enquiry into the Crafts in Australia (Bonython) 1975
- Industries Assistance Commission Inquiry into Assistance to the Performing Arts 1976
- Senate Standing Committee on Education and the Arts Report on Employment of Musicians by the Australian Broadcasting Commission 1977
- Task Force on Education and the Arts for Young People (Boomer) 1984
- Study into the Future Development of Orchestras in Australia (Tribe) 1985
- Commonwealth Tertiary Education Commission Review of Arts Education and Training (Botsman)
- House of Representatives Standing Committee on Expenditure (McLeay) 1986
- Committee of Inquiry into Folklife in Australia (Anderson) 1987
- Review of Aboriginal Arts and Craft Industry (Altman) 1989
- Major Performing Arts Inquiry (Nugent) 1999
- Report of the Contemporary Visual Arts and Crafts Inquiry (Myer) 2002
- Cultural Minister Council : Report on an Examination of the Small to Medium Performing Arts Sector 2002
- Review of the National Museum of Australia—Its Exhibitions and Public Programs (Carroll) 2003
- Review of Australia's Symphony and Pit Orchestras (Strong) 2005
- Senate Standing Committee on Environment, Information Technology and the Arts Inquiry into Australia's Indigenous Visual arts and crafts sector (Eggleston) 2007
- Review of the National Academy of Music (currently under way).

Readers' Forum

Responses to Peter Rechniewski's *The Permanent Underground: Australian Contemporary Jazz in the New Millennium*

Tony Mitchell teaches cultural studies and popular music at the University of Technology, Sydney. Author of *Popular Music and Local Identity: Pop, Rock and Rap in Europe and Oceania* (1996), he is currently working on *Local Noise* (localnoise.net.au), an ARC-funded project on Australasian hip hop.

In my opinion, Peter Rechniewski over-dramatizes the neglect of Australian jazz in the media and elsewhere, and his prognosis amounts to a stultifying attempt to institutionalize it as a mainstream activity. Although I cannot speak as an 'insider', I am a music and cultural studies lecturer and researcher with a considerable collection of Australian jazz CDs, a regular listener to 'Jazz Track', and I frequently go to local jazz gigs, especially those by the Necks and related groups. I do consider myself to be an expert on Australian hip hop, which I have researched and written about over the past 10 years, and which—to its credit—occupies a niche much further 'underground' in Australian music than jazz does, and which has occasionally interacted with the Sydney jazz scene through groups such as Hermitage, Upshot and Good Buddha.

My impression is that, although Australian jazz has on the whole not achieved mainstream success locally (thankfully), and despite being 'weak, lacking in financial means and fragmented' (PP16, p. 45), it is thriving in terms of a prevailing sense of innovation, resilience, experimentation and diversity—which run the risk of being stifled by Rechniewski's 'modest plan'. An unfortunate aspect of Rechniewski's argument is that he insists on denigrating what he refers to as 'rock/pop', a meaningless category which presumably covers any kind of music that is not rigidly contained within art/classical or jazz parameters. One group he uses to exemplify the international recognition Australian jazz has received is the Necks, who, largely due to being regularly featured in British avant-garde style bible *The Wire*, have received considerable acclaim throughout Europe. But, according to Rechniewski, the Necks 'could not possibly be considered experimental or under-exposed' (p. 34). Indeed, they could not possibly be considered a jazz group either, as their music transcends boundaries, incorporating trance, minimalism, rock, classical and avant-garde. Yet the Necks have received little, if any, government funding for their music here, and in order to survive rely largely on the considerable versatility of their members in related music genres such as rock and avant-garde (pianist Chris Abrahams), jazz, dub and rock (Lloyd Swanton), and the Japanese, European and US avant-garde (Tony Buck). They exemplify what has become a widespread network of musical diversity in the Sydney jazz scene—being Sydney-based, admittedly I don't get to hear much live jazz from elsewhere in Australia—where most local musicians play in a variety of different groups and combinations, often crossing different genres.

One really has to wonder what Rechniewski regards as 'experimental' in Australian jazz, given his grotesque suggestion of a 'jazz and new music' series involving Ten Part Invention, Chris Abrahams, Scott Tinkler, the John Butler Trio, and Tim Friedman of the Whitlams. Throw in Katie Noonan and John Farnham and we'd have a real freak show – a ridiculously watered-down 'experimental' attempt to combine jazz and mainstream pop in a misguided kind of crossover that gives all involved a bad name. Of course, there are enduring stereotypes associated with the term 'jazz'—the trad band of elderly gents in white suits and straw hats springs to mind—which give it somewhat daggy overtones. But surely it has always been a bastard form, cannibalising other genres of music, and forging paths of improvisation, ingenuity and surprise which break boundaries of music genre. The recent sold-out concerts by Ornette Coleman and Sonny Rollins at the Sydney Opera House—the latter very ably, if only briefly, supported by Mike Nock—suggest that there may even be a mainstream audience for innovative, experimental jazz which attempts at institutionalisation will surely not help to flourish at all.

Kate Lidbetter is Director of Music at the Australia Council.

Peter Rechniewski offers a timely analysis of the Australian contemporary jazz and improvisation scene. His Platform Paper raises an important issue for the sector – will the creation of a national jazz plan assist the key stakeholders in providing better opportunities for jazz musicians, audiences and service providers? The Music Board of the Australia Council for the Arts believes it will.

In his paper, Peter acknowledges that the jazz sector has been historically divided, and calls for his colleagues to end their rivalry and work together. Over recent months I have witnessed a united approach and am delighted to work with some of the key proponents of a jazz plan.

The Australia Council has convened two national jazz forums in recent years – the first at the 2006 Wangaratta Festival of Jazz, and a second in late 2007 in Sydney. Predominantly attended by recipients (both individuals and organisations) of Music Board funding, these forums dwelled mainly on three issues—the future of the national jazz website (www.jazzaustralia.com.au), the benefits of a national network of jazz service organisations, and opportunities for national touring circuits. A real spirit of collaboration was evident at these forums and the outcomes have been positive.

Following discussion and consultation with the sector, the Music Board has committed a further $25,000 towards the redevelopment of the site. Applications for this redevelopment have now closed, and a steering committee of representatives from the forums aims to launch the new site at the 2008 Wangaratta Festival of Jazz. The site will be revitalised, energised, and self-sufficient.

New national touring opportunities have also opened up with a new initiative called Sound Travellers (www.soundtravellers.com.au). This project, funded by the Australia Council, is managed by Ceres Solutions and Performing Lines and provides assistance to new music practitioners touring interstate. A number of jazz tours have been supported in its first round of funding and the initiative has been seen as a positive move that will facilitate some tours that would otherwise not have occurred.

A third important outcome has been the creation of a national jazz development officer (NJDO). This is the first step towards the national jazz plan that Peter calls for in his Platform Paper. The Music Board invested $30,000 and SIMA has agreed to auspice the grant and co-ordinate the recruitment process on behalf of the broader group that attended the forum. It is expected that the NJDO will undertake research into existing services, venues, infrastructure and support for jazz musicians; draft a national jazz plan for the period 2009–2011; oversee the redevelopment of the website; and seek further funding partners to continue the role into the future. Obviously all of this will be done in consultation and collaboration with the jazz sector, and the same steering committee that has generously taken on the role of overseeing the website development will also work closely with the NJDO.

These are really positive, substantial outcomes that came as a result of a group of passionate advocates for jazz having an open and constructive discussion. Not everyone will agree with every outcome or every recommendation made by the jazz plan. It's inevitable that what one group advocates, another may dismiss. But I am optimistic that this is a great moment for Australian jazz, and that when the sector speaks with a united, informed and persuasive voice, it will achieve its goals. The Music Board is excited to be one of the partners that will assist that outcome.